Testimonials

Ellen is our dental "angel" advocate. Her book exposes all the murky and sometimes secretive details of the dental industry, such as fillings, root canals, crowns, implants, dentures, and more, and the expenses and insurance involved. She presents the information in such an easy to read and informative manner that it's not possible any longer to wonder whether to trust a dental professional or his/her treatment or not. Hooray for Ellen Broyles! I can honestly say that I appreciate her writing this book; the information has been kept under cover for too long. Thanks, Ellen. – Terry Mills

Ellen the book is great! I sat down to just read a chapter or two and ended up finishing it because it was so fun, definitely not the typical, dry literature you'd read about a medical profession! The structure and content were perfect. Thanks for sending me along a copy; I think it's a great idea to educate patients! - Casey Caraher

Ellen has personally saved our family thousands of dollars by intercepting treatment plans that would have drained our bank accounts. We can't thank her enough for her time and caring attitude for us and many of our other family members that have gone to her for dental advocacy. She was able to inform us with alternative suggestions and refer us to other dentists that were able to provide them. - Marcy Dodds

My sister was in severe dental pain one evening; we were referred to Ellen to help us find available dental resources and she was able to find a clinic that worked on a sliding fee schedule. Both my sister and I thank you Ellen! Thanks to your recommendation, she received wonderful dental care that she could afford! Thank you again,- Debby Cabales

I have always called Ellen over the years to get a second opinion of the treatment plan I received from various dentists. She has always been able to either agree with the dentist's plan of treatment or disagree offering viable options for me. I will continue to ask her advice when it comes to hard decisions with my dental treatment. - Nancy White

My cousin was in dire need of dental help Not only did she lack the funds for dental treatment but she was very scared of dentists in general. Not only did Ellen take the time to find her an adequate but inexpensive dental insurance plan for her, but she also found her a very empathetic dentist to work with Gwen. Ellen even brought her to her first appointment so she would feel more comfortable. Thank you, Ellen – Kim Ledgerwood

THE
DENTAL PATIENT'S
SURVIVAL GUIDE™

FROM AN INSIDERS VIEW

ELLEN BROYLES

For more survival tips visit The Dental Patient's
Survival Guide companion website at
www.survivingthedentist.com

iUniverse, Inc.
Bloomington

THE DENTAL PATIENT'S SURVIVAL GUIDE™ FROM AN INSIDERS VIEW

Copyright © 2011 by Ellen Broyles

iUniverse books may be ordered through booksellers or by contacting:

iUniverse
1663 Liberty Drive
Bloomington, IN 47403
www.iuniverse.com
1-800-Authors (1-800-288-4677)

Because of the dynamic nature of the Internet, any web addresses or links contained in this book may have changed since publication and may no longer be valid. The views expressed in this work are solely those of the author and do not necessarily reflect the views of the publisher, and the publisher hereby disclaims any responsibility for them.

Any people depicted in stock imagery provided by Thinkstock are models, and such images are being used for illustrative purposes only.

Certain stock imagery © Thinkstock.

ISBN: 978-1-4620-1286-2 (sc)
ISBN: 978-1-4620-1287-9 (ebk)

Printed in the United States of America

iUniverse rev. date: 05/09/2011

TABLE OF CONTENTS

Acknowledgements

I have so many people in my life to thank for encouraging me to actually make this happen. First, I have to thank my husband of 31 years for listening to all of my endless dental stories with great interest (even if he was probably just pretending).

To both of my son's, Nathan and Daniel, who have given me great joy for many years. Nathan my very techy son, is my own personal graphic designer and my go to person for any technical advise regarding my project. Daniel has always cheered me on by a "You can do it Mom!" support person. Thank you to their lovely wives Nicole and Lindy who somehow manage to put up with my many phone calls checking on everyone and asking for feedback on my project.

Also Corry Damey, my artist who hand drew all of the great visuals that are throughout the book. Corry arrived on the scene towards the end of my project with some really great ideas. Thank you, Corry.

I must also mention Dr. Dan Broughton, D.D.S., who has been my mentor, consultant, and support person. He has encouraged me to continue this project until finished. Thank you, Dr. Dan, for all the years you've given to the dental field and the countless number of people that you have helped!

Are you going to the dentist? Do you know anything about dentistry? Would you like to be informed and go in with some knowledge? I know I would like that!

CHAPTER 1

AMALGAM VS. COMPOSITE
Silver Fillings vs. White Fillings
The Myths, The Pros, The Cons

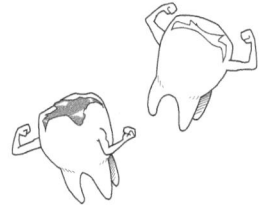

- Many physicians and dentists have given testimonies about amalgam (**silver fillings**) regarding the false accusations of their dangers.
  See the "Mercury Toxicity Scam," also "How Anti-Amalgamists Swindle People" by Stephen Barrett, M.D., under "Quackwatch" on the web for just a few of these testimonials.

- Many dentists have used this scare tactic in the past, so that they can perform unnecessary, costly dental treatment for their patients. Many continue to do it today. They advise patients to replace all their silver amalgam fillings with **composite fillings**. This can lead to the dental patient spending thousands of dollars when in fact there has never been a study done on the expensive white composite fillings materials and their possible role in causing harmful effects on the body. Amalgam fillings can last years longer than their composite counterparts.

- The insurance companies do not recognize the com- 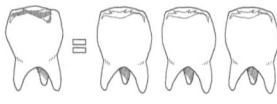 posite fillings as a neces- sity in the posterior teeth (molars and bicuspids). Therefore, they pay a substantially lesser amount when they have one done in the posterior teeth costing them much more out of pocket.

- Now for the pros of composite filling materials(white), there is no doubt they esthetically look much better than the silver amalgams. The composite materials now have many shades available to match your own tooth color perfectly.

- My final analysis for the amalgam vs. composite is this: If you have unlimited funds and time to spend in the dental chair, feel free to purchase the composite fillings. However, don't ever let a dentist talk you out of removing all your silver fillings using scare tactics to replace them with expensive composite fillings. Save your money for the anterior teeth (cuspid to cuspid). The insurance will allow maximum compensation for these.

CHAPTER 2

HELP! THE $5000.00 TREATMENT PLAN

You have just come out of the dental office, and you are completely dazed and confused about the information you have received! If you get nothing else out of this chapter, always, always get a second (possibly third) opinion on anything $1,000.00 and above. I have never seen in my entire career as a dental advocate such 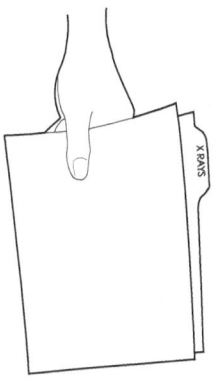 an enormous difference in the fees that dentists are charging for the same procedure. Dentists are always more then happy to give you a free consultation and opinion regarding treatment. Be sure and ask for your dental X-rays that you just had done so you can bring them with you to your second opinion appointment. Then you won't have to pay for any additional X-rays.

Many dentists differ on whether a tooth needs a crown or a filling. Your more conservative dentist will always advise a filling if it's at all possible. There are several different criteria in the deciding factor. How large is the existing filling? Is the tooth cracked? Does it have or need a root canal. If it's an existing small to medium filling, ask the dentist to replace it with another filling. If it's a large filling, and you don't have the funds for a crown at the moment, ask the dentist to remove the decay and do a build-up or stainless steel crown on the tooth until you have the funds available (usually they have to do a build-up anyway so the crown has a strong structure to sit on). Now, keep in mind, a build-up is a very large filling placed on the tooth, and it can be 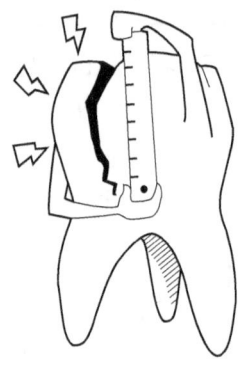 either composite or amalgam. If you opt for this, the tooth is at risk for breakage if you chew something hard on it, i.e. hard candy, peanut brittle, etc., so you want to just be aware of it. I have seen many build-ups last for years without a problem. Another option is to place a temporary crown or stainless steel crown (I've seen these last two to three years, or even longer) while waiting for more funds to come in. If you have a root canal on a tooth, it will cut off the blood supply to the tooth causing the tooth to become brittle and vulnerable to breakage, so if you are willing to put the finances in it for the root canal, you need to place a permanent or temporary crown on it as soon as possible.

The last option, which I never like to recommend but is sometimes necessary, is the extraction or removal of a tooth.

BE SURE AND THINK ABOUT THE FOLLOWING WHEN DECIDING ON TREATMENT:

- Did the dentist see you on an emergency basis and tell you to sink $3,000 into one tooth without looking  at the whole picture? There is no sense in wasting money on one tooth when there are many others that are in need of help, possibly more important teeth. I have spoken to many patients that have been told to have expensive dental treatment done without understanding the pros or cons of saving a tooth. It may be that it's a very back molar that has no opposing tooth, but the dentist is advising you to save it at a very high cost. But why? What is the reason?

- Do not make any rash decisions when talking about this much money. Insurance maximums average about $1,500 per year so there goes all your insurance for the year on one tooth. You always want to have the dentist look at the bone level and gum tissue as well. The tooth may not be worth saving.

- If you have an existing denture that does not fit anymore, but you can't afford a new denture at this time, ask the dentist if they can do a softline or a chairside hardliner for the denture. This may buy you some time and stabilize the denture for a while.

- If you have a missing front tooth, ask the dentist about a "Flipper." This is an inexpensive removable device that will replace your front tooth.

CHAPTER 3

GET OUT OF PAIN QUICK!!

Most of us have been in that horrible situation where we've been in extreme pain and will do just about any-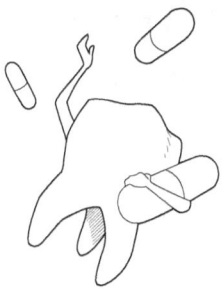thing to get help. This is when we are at our most vulnerable, and we need not make any important decisions until we can think clearly again. I am going to list a few scenarios that will help stabilize the "Hot Tooth Syndrome."

- Throbbing pain, waking at night with tooth pain, sensitivity to warm liquids, cold liquids seeming to be more soothing, and swelling in gum tissue above the throbbing tooth. These are all hallmark conditions of a tooth that has an abscess/dying nerve. To get the tooth to calm down quickly get to your dentist and get on a course of antibiotics. (If it's the weekend and you cannot reach your dentist and/or don't have one at all, you can go to the hospital, and they will get you a prescription of antibiotics.) Take the full course of the antibiotic. After the first day it should start calming down. Do not make the mistake most people do and after the toothache is gone they will procrastinate and not follow up with a visit to the dentist to get it taken care of. You will sooner than later have another horrendous toothache.

- A dentist can also do what they call an "Open and Broach" where they will open the tooth, quickly drain and clean the roots and temporize it until a root canal 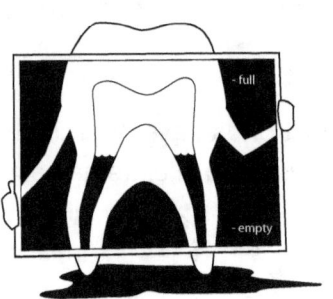 can be completed on it. This scenario can be used if you want to save the tooth but don't have the funds right now for a complete root canal. Let's say it's towards the end of the year, and you've maximized your insurance for the year, and you want to have the root canal completed when your insurance funds will be renewed. In this case I have seen the "Open and Broach" method used to get patients by many times until the new year starts so they can have their full coverage.

- It may be a cracked tooth which can also cause extreme pain. If that is the case and it is cracked below the bone and the gum line, it will need to be removed. If the crack doesn't go down that far, the dentist can place a crown on it and/or temporary crown it until you have funds to pay for it.

- I have also seen patients have pain after a filling/ crown has been done because it's too high and the bite is uneven. It's being pounded on by the opposing tooth. YOU MUST get back into the dentist and have them adjust the bite. It only takes a few minutes and is a very easy fix, but if you let it go that way I've seen it destroy the nerve of the tooth and crack either the tooth with the new filling or the opposing tooth that it's hitting on too hard.

Once you are out of pain, you can then discuss calmly what needs to be done to completely restore the tooth, the cost involved, and what will the insurance cover.

CHAPTER 4

I AM FIRING MY DENTIST!

Here are a few things to look for and to be wary of when you are looking for a new dentist or are having second thoughts about your existing dentist:

- Staff longevity is very important. If you see a huge  turnover in staff, whether it be reception, dental assistant, or hygienist, something is not right with the dentist. It is a sure sign that the dentist isn't treating his patients or staff right. Neither scenario is good, and I would look for a new dentist.

- Be wary of the name of the dental practice. If you see a name like "Cosmetic Dentistry Practice," you will see the price tag go up at least three times for the exact same procedure that any other general dentist can give you. There is no special training required, nor are there any special materials required.

- Red flags also go up when a practice touts "Natural Therapy Dentistry." Again, the price tag goes way up on the same procedures and the same materials that every other dentist has. They will definitely be the ones that will use all the scare tactics to remove all the amalgams and replace them with composites even though, as I stated earlier, there has been no study on composite materials and how they can affect the body.

- Don't let a dentist talk you into expensive "In Office Bleaching." Retail store dental bleaching products

are currently just as good, and many dental offices are offering free bleaching trays and materials for life if you come in for the regular exam, cleaning, and X-rays.

- The staff needs to be friendly and helpful. Staff includes front office scheduling coordinator, insurance specialist, dental assistant, dental hygienist, and dentist. All members should be able to support what the dentist is recommending for your dental needs. Ask them if you were their mother or father, if they would back up what the dentist is telling you. The dentist should be able to communicate to the front office and yourself what's priority and what can be on hold. It is their job to know what your insurance is all about. Your treatment plan should be spread out so you can do so much every year in order to maximize your insurance benefits. This way you will minimize your out-of-pocket expenses.

- I would definitely find a dental office that employs a dental hygienist for your dental cleaning. They usually do a much better cleaning than the dentist because this is their specific training and what they do eight hours a day. Regular dental cleanings are just as important as any other dental procedure. If you don't have healthy gums and bone level, no matter how great the teeth are, they will lose the foundation they need. (Sorry, dentists. You're better at fillings and crowns and bridges. Let the hygienist do his/her job.)

- The dentist should be willing to redo any treatment that you are not happy with within a realistic amount of time that it was completed. A crown needs to last a minimum of five years. Fillings need to last a 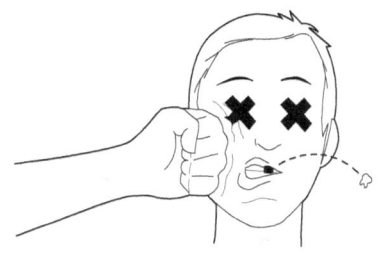 minimum of three years because insurance will not cover another crown or filling before that. I would not hesitate to go back to the dentist who completed the treatment originally so they can determine what happened, and many times they will redo it at no charge. (There are always exceptions. However, if you participate in a fist fight and get some of your beautiful teeth knocked out or fractured, this does not fall into the "redo at no charge category"! Also, you must take good care of your teeth. If you don't brush and floss regularly, the dental work will break down much faster, and you can hardly blame that on the dentist.

- Remember when seeing a specialist or general dentist of any kind, always go in for a consultation first to understand what the treatment will be, and know the expense ahead of time so you are prepared. Any, and I mean _any_, office should be able to tell you exactly what your insurance will cover and what your out-of- pocket expense will be. IF they can't offer that assistance to you, raise your red flag and go get another opinion!

CHAPTER 5

WHEN TO SEE A SPECIALIST

In this chapter I will touch base on a few of the different specialists that are available and when you should go see one:

- The Oral Surgeon: I have worked as an oral surgery assistant and would recommend if at all possible see one for any extraction unless it is a very simple extraction. They may cost more but they are worth it. Some of the general dentists I have worked with have spent hours trying to remove a tooth when an oral surgeon can do it in minutes without causing all of the trauma to the surrounding area, i.e. bone and tissue. Always see an oral surgeon for these situations: wisdom teeth removal, an impacted tooth, and a tooth that is broken down by decay which will usually break apart and take hours to remove if it is not done by an expert. One more advantage is that an oral surgeon will have the training and the equipment to place patients under general anesthetic.

- The Periodontist: The gums are just as important to take care of as the teeth are because if you don't have great gum and bone support, your teeth will eventually fall out. A knowledgeable hygienist will go around the entire mouth and take the measurements of gum line pocket depth (that 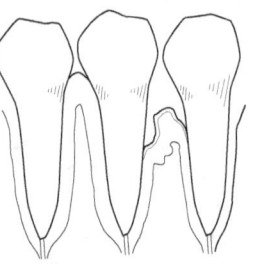 is when you hear her report the numbers 232,322, etc.) This should be done at least once a year. If you have numbers going as far as four on up, you should get a consultation with a periodontist. Again, most specialists will offer free consultations, so it is always worthwhile to pursue that when dealing with something as important as your dental health.

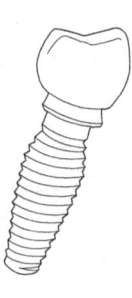 • The Periodontist and the Oral Surgeon: Never let a general dentist perform an implant procedure. I don't care if it's $1,000 dollars cheaper! I have seen several tout they can do this, but they never last. This is a highly technical procedure which requires the extra training of a specialist.

• The Orthodontist: Never go to a general dentist for orthodontic care. This is definitely a very specialized field a general dentist should not mess with. The price might sound much better, but in the end you usually have to see the expert to fix what the general dentist messed up. Also, I have to mention Invisalign Technology. This is ONLY for very easy orthodontic cases. You might need just a little tweak here or there. For any other complex case you still need to go into regular braces, otherwise you will spend the rest of your life wearing Invisalign trays and spending much more money.

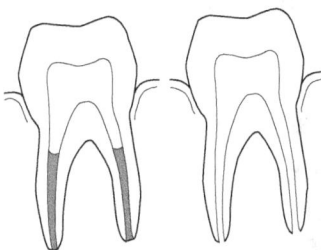

•   The Endodontist (Root Canal Specialist): It used to be much more common for the general dentist to do root canals on teeth when needed. However, more and more dentists are sending their root canal patients to the specialist. I do believe if a general dentist does root canals routinely, they can be fine. Saying that I want to point out the advantages of seeing an endodontist for your root canal. They have special training, special equipment that speeds up the process tremendously, and very expensive scopes and materials that general dentists can't offer. In making the decision ask yourself this: Can I afford a specialist? Ask the front office staff what your part will be after insurance covers its part.

•   The Prosthodontist (Specializes in Complex Dentures, Crowns, Bridges and Jaw/Joint problems.): Only the most difficult cases are sent to a prosthodontist. By that I mean they have a difficult bite for a denture or their jaw is having severe pain issues. The general dentist should be able to produce a great fitting denture and or a partial denture.

- The Pedodontist (Children's Specialist): Most general dentists and staff are great with kids. If a child is not manageable, he or she is referred to a pedodontist. The majority of children do just fine in a regular setting, and it is not necessary to spend the extra money to see a specialist. Start your child off very young, age two, with a visit to your dental office for a ride  in the chair, a peek at the teeth with the tiny mirror, and a little gift bag for coming in. They will have great memories of the dental office and won't be scared to come in again.

CHAPTER 6

BRIDGES, CROWNS AND IMPLANTS, OH MY!

In this chapter I will explain why, what, and where for the most expensive dental treatments.

Why do you need a dental bridge?

- Simple--a tooth is missing in between two other teeth. Again, I've seen costs on crowns or bridges range anywhere from $3,000 to $10,000 for a three-unit bridge (that is crowning each tooth on either side, and the crown in the middle replacing the missing tooth). Be carful of your insurance because this must always be preauthorized before you have this expensive procedure done. Sometimes insurances have what they call "a missing tooth clause" where if you were missing the tooth prior to coverage, they won't pay anything to replace it.

- Implant or bridge? A three-unit bridge is approximately the same cost as an implant and crown, so look at these following criteria

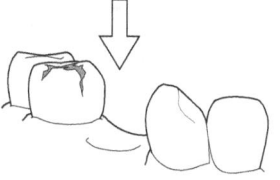

when considering which one you want: Are the teeth on either side of the missing tooth filling free? If so, the implant is a better way to go. Why destroy perfect tooth structure and cover it with crowns when an implant is the same cost and can be done with one crown. If the existing teeth by the missing tooth have moderate to large existing fillings, than by all means choose the bridge because eventually you will probably need to replace those fillings with crowns anyway.

- Let's say you are missing a tooth but don't have the funds to replace it right away. Ask the dentist for what they call a "flipper." It is a removable temporary partial that will replace the tooth at a fraction of the cost and can be a temporary fix for a long time if necessary. It will save the space for a future bridge so the teeth don't drift as well.

- If it is a back tooth and you don't want to replace it, that is also an option, and many patients have chosen that. The down side on 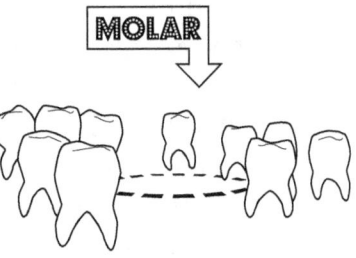 that scenario is that the remaining teeth can drift without that permanent holding everything in its space. However, this takes years.

- Bridges, crowns and implants are all permanent fixtures. The bridges and crowns are cemented in, and the implant is surgically embedded into the bone, and a crown is placed on top. When considering an implant, know that they take several months to complete so you spend more time in the dental chair.

- If you have an existing crown or bridge that is loose, ask the dentist if he can gently tap it off, clean it out, and re-cement it. If the tooth and crown are intact, this is a very inexpensive and a best case scenario for the patient. Also, there are miniature ratchets and screws to help remove a crown, so it is not destroyed. It's always much better for the patient in terms of cost and time to use the existing crown when possible.

Also, guess what, if you decide you can get along just fine without it and you've been advised of why you should have it replaced verses leaving it alone, don't feel like anything is going to happen over night. Sometimes the dentist can send out false alarming messages out to patients. They can make the patient feel as if their whole life as they know it will come to an end if they don't come up with thousands of dollars immediately to fix it. NO! NO! NO! If you feel like you are being pressured, a red flag should go up!!! Go elsewhere!

CHAPTER 7

JUST FOR KIDS

Prevention, prevention, prevention is what I preach when dealing with the children. Watch their diet, not a lot of sugars, sodas and not walking around with the baby bottle filled with apple juice. Mom and Dad, you have to help your younger child to brush and floss at least two times per day as they don't have the dexterity it takes to do a good job of it. Make sure they get into the dentist every six months for their cleaning and checkup.

Start taking them in at one to two years old just for a ride in the chair and some cute little toys and toothbrush. If your child is introduced to the dental world at an early age, it will save you from having to go to an expensive children's specialist office (pedodontist) as they will not be apprehensive about being there the more you bring them in. Let the younger sibling go

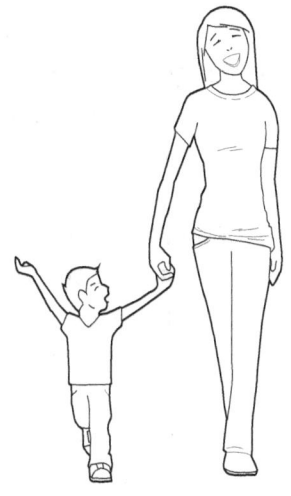

with the older child so they can see how fun the cleanings are, and they will look forward to their turn in the chair.

WHAT ABOUT FLUORIDE?

The body uses many building blocks to form body parts. As teeth form, FLUORIDE is a very important building block! If fluoride is not available in the body, substitutes are used. The critical ages for fluoride to be used, is from birth to approximately ten years of age. Sources for fluoride: most municipal water supplies (one part per million). Pediatric vitamins can include fluoride in the prescription. Dentists can provide prescriptions for fluoride drops or tablets. Bottled water doesn't contain fluoride. Most well water in the Northwest does not contain fluoride.

What about my child's "Bucky Beaver" teeth? At about age seven, children begin acquiring full size, adult front teeth (incisors). Because these teeth are adult- size, and the child's face is still child-size, it is normal to have large, crowded teeth in a small face for three or four years. As the bones of the face and jaws grow to accommodate the teeth, the face becomes more adult in appearance. Orthodontic treatment is rarely needed in this period of growth. Around age twelve is usually the best age to determine if there is a need for orthodontic treatment. Mother nature's patterns are well established. Give her a chance

As children get older make sure they get their sealants done on all there permanent molars. This is one of the best preventative measures a child can have. Sealants can stop small areas of decay from becoming larger. Clinical studies have confirmed that properly placed sealants, if kept intact, will stop decay in the enamel. AND IT IS SO EASY TO APPLY! The sealant is just painted on. Also, it is very inexpensive compared to a permanent filling.

I recommend fluoride for children. Many cities already have fluoride in the water. If not, you can get fluoride drops from the dentist. Fluoride will make the teeth stronger and less susceptible to decay. Your dental office should place fluoride on the teeth after they are polished. Now they have a type of fluoride that you can just paint on the teeth, and it is very easy for the little patient to handle it.

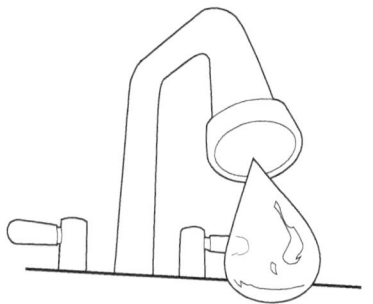

CHAPTER 8

THE TRUTH ABOUT DENTURES AND PARTIAL DENTURES

This should be the last resort!!! Don't ever let a dentist tell you how great everything will be when you have dentures (if they are so great why are the drug stores full of "stickum" remedies)! That is usually the beginning of a long road of adjusting to a new way to talking and eating. I don't want to go overboard on this issue because for some people this is the only option for them. I am talking to the patient that comes in, as I have seen numerous times, and begs the dentist for dentures. The patient is tired of dealing with dental work and dental bills, and all he can think of is how great it would be to escape all that time and treatment in the dental chair. The patient that has this mindset is going to have a rude awakening. Not one patient in the 25 years who has come in and gone through with the

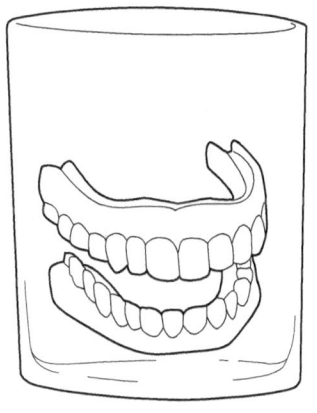

dentures has been happy with the outcome. (I even had one patient blame his full dentures on ruining his sex life). They will automatically be very upset with the dentist for doing the dentures for them in the first place even though they pleaded to have it done. If there is no other option fine, but very rarely is that the case. When getting prepared for full dentures you must always get the patient prepared for what lies ahead. If the dentist does that, the outcome will be so much better mentally and physically for the patient.

The patient needs to be told about these real problems that they will experience when they first get their full dentures.

- You will need to relearn to talk. The most expedient way is to read a book out loud when home.

- You will need to learn how to chew again.

Blah Blah Blah...

- The taste of food will not be the same. You will lose some of the flavor of food.

- You will experience "sore spots" which is normal! Many pa-tients feel as if they are complainers and go away and not wear them. You will need to go in for adjustments for the first four to five weeks, maybe more. This should be done at no charge and is normally included in the cost of the new denture or partial denture. If it isn't get another consultation.

If you make the patient aware of these challenges they will accept the dentures much easier and get used to them much quicker than the patient who thinks it's all going to be wonderful.

If you can get away with a partial denture, that is even better. With a partial denture you can keep the teeth that are worth saving, and the partial will replace the missing teeth in your mouth. Don't get me wrong-- it's still not a piece of cake. It's still removable, and you have to get used to all of the above points that I mentioned with a full denture, but it's always better to save any teeth if possible.

CHAPTER 9

DENTAL FEES

I have never witnessed another time in my career when the fees of each dental office can vary so much. That is why I always recommend searching out a second and third opinion, especially when discussing crowns, bridges, or any of the more expensive dental procedures. I have seen different dental procedures fees change from office to office by several hundred  dollars, sometimes even more. Depending on the area, these fees can vary slightly but shouldn't be a huge difference in cost. At the end of your exam visit you should receive a printout of your treatment plan and costs. If you are uncomfortable with the prices at all, just call a few offices and compare. The office that is friendly and has a great environment should make you feel very comfortable and give you the information freely. If they have an attitude about taking the time to help you, that is another red flag, and you can skip that office.

CHAPTER 10

CLINICS THAT WILL WORK ON A SLIDING FEE SCALE AND HOW TO FIND ONE

Call your local Department of Social and Human Services and ask if they can refer you to a Public Health Dental Clinic close to your area. They usually can provide lists for the state you're in for all of the community dental offices that will work on a sliding fee scale (or for no charge at all depending on your circumstances). You can also contact your local Dental Society Office for advice on clinics that offer dental care at low costs. Contact your local college that offer dental degrees and local technical community college that have hygiene and dental assistant programs. They will usually have an onsite clinic where you can get your dental work done for much less. Children up to age eighteen will usually always be able to receive state assistance for their dental treatment. Never feel like you are receiving second rate dental care in this environment. I have worked for the schools and volunteered at many of the low income clinics, and dental staff are just as professional and caring as in any regular dental office.

CHAPTER 11

I DON'T UNDERSTAND MY DENTAL INSURANCE. HELP!

It would be truly amiss of me not to mention the wonderful world of dental insurance. I have worked closely with dental insurance for the last three years of my dental career, and it's a wonder I'm still half-way sane, although some would argue that. So, this chapter is dedicated to all of those dental office insurance coordinators that have to deal with insurance everyday. Consider them dental insurance angels! I understand patients that come in swearing on the Bible that they are covered by such and such plan and all their children are covered as well. When in the end the poor misinformed patient finds out it's really just his/her medical plan **or** all the insurance was dropped due to the fact he/she didn't sign the contracts at work on time **or** he/she has been carrying around the old dental insurance card that's been stuck in his/her wallet for the last ten years, and they missed the H.R. meeting where all there insurance has been changed to another carrier. Meanwhile the dental receptionist has submitted the insurance to three different places all denied, denied, denied. Dental patients, be kind and considerate to this person because if this person is doing their job right, they can get the payments that your insurance tries to deny albeit takes quite a lot of effort in some cases. I have taken on the more complex cases when insurance tries to deny payment on claims. Sometimes it's as simple as calling the insurance company to remind them this is what the patient is paying for every month, and if they don't pay for the claim, I will be in touch with the Insurance Commissioner. I usually get payment using this tactic within the next few days. The dental office insurance person MUST be your advocate when dealing with insurance problems. They must take the time, which in many cases starts with thirty minutes on hold, before you can talk to a real person. It is the insurance person's responsibility to fight for your rights because they should have the background and understanding of dental treatment and insurance to do so. If they don't, the dentist has the responsibility to hire someone that is insurance savvy.

This is a list of items your dental front office staff should be able to help you with:

- If you are on a P.P.O. Plan, call and ask the front office staff whether they are on your list of contracted dentists.

- The front office staff should call your insurance the minute you make the appointment and gather all of your insurance plan information in detail. When you walk through the door, they will know exactly what your maximum is and what percentage your insurance will pay on each and every procedure.

- The staff will know if your family is covered. For example, will you have a "Missing Tooth Clause"? This is very important to find out because many patients have been sticker shocked to receive a bill being totally responsible for the $4,095 fee because no one checked on this issue.

- The staff mem-
ber should be
able to sit down
with you after
the dentist has
given you this
enormous treat-
ment plan (your
head is spinning
with thoughts of Dentures, don't go there!!!) say "It's okay let's go over everything, prioritize and plan a year by year treatment plan. The treatment coordinator should also be able to go over all the treatment step by step, show pictures and take the time to help you understand exactly what you need and why. Many times the patient feels much more comfortable talking to a staff member and asking questions about why and going over alternatives that are possible. Its okay you don't have to do everything overnight. If the dentist is pushing you into a large treatment plan that costs thousands and it

needs to be done right away consider it a red flag issue and get your second opinion. Remember it took a long time for your teeth to get into this condition and it's fine to work on it a little at a time. I've seen many patients so upset and distraught over a huge amount of work that needs to be done that it overwhelms them and they end up running out of the office not doing anything.

- Remember each year you can complete so much of the recommended treatment utilizing your benefits to the maximum and again minimizing your out of pocket expenses.

- The staff will be able to tell you exactly what your patient portion will be before each appointment and give you a typed treatment plan with what your insurance will pay and what your part will be.

One final comment regarding Dental Insurance, take note that Dental Insurance Maximums are basically the same as when I first started in this industry 25 years ago. When I began the maximum was $1,000 per year, today 25 years later the average maximum is $1,500 per year. The Dental Fees have gone up more than 5x that of the Dental Insurance maximums. Therefore the dental patient can use their whole maximum on just one tooth and that will be it for the year. Someone really needs to take the dental insurance companies to task on this issue.

FINAL COMMENTS

I hope I have been able to help everyone with your own dental dilemma.

Every employee of a dental office should be able to ask themselves ONE question: if this was my family member, is this what I would still be recommending for them and have that answer be an undeniable "YES."

Dentists don't make the staff push dental work that doesn't need to be done. I have met many dental auxiliary staff that have quit just for that reason. Give the patients the Cadillac treatment plan but always offer alternatives for those expensive procedures.

Hire qualified dental personnel, pay them what they're worth, and you won't need to micromanage your staff. You and your patients' lives will run much smoother.

A dental office should have a comfortable atmosphere. Don't try to mass produce dental treatment; it makes for a very hectic day.

The office should have a knowledgeable treatment coordinator so the hygienist, dentist, and dental assistant can all work at a balanced pace throughout the day. The patients and the staff all have time to say a few words before treatment begins. This is very important in practice building!

GLOSSARY

Abscess: localized inflammation, with a collection of pus, usually swelling

Amalgam: The silver filling material used primarily in posterior teeth. It consists of a metal alloy of silver, tin, zinc and copper combined with mercury.

Anterior Teeth: The six upper or six lower front teeth

Antibiotic: Any substance produced by a microorganism which harms or kills another microorganism.

Apex: The tip of a root of a tooth.

Apicoectomy: removal of the root end of a tooth to treat an infection

Asymptomatic: A lack of symptoms or complaints by the patient.

Bleaching: The technique of applying a chemical agent, usually hydrogen peroxide, to the teeth to whiten them.

Braces: devices used by orthodontists to gradually reposition teeth to a more favorable alignment

Dental Bridge: replaces one or more missing teeth, cemented or bonded to supporting teeth or implants adjacent to the space

Calculus: The hard residue that forms on teeth due to plaque buildup, often stained yellow or brown; also known as tartar

Cavities: A decay lesion or hole in a tooth

Cavitron: dental tool that uses high frequency sound waves to clean teeth

Composite Filling: Tooth colored filling. Insurance companies usually only allow them on the front teeth (anterior teeth). When composites are done on the back teeth (posterior teeth) the insurance company usually pays them as an amalgam.

Crown: A metal, plastic or porcelain restoration that covers the whole crown of the tooth. Sometimes called a cap.

Decay: the lay term for carious lesions in a tooth; decomposition of tooth structure

Dental Hygienist: A dental professional who specializes in cleaning the teeth by removing plaque, calculus, and diseased gum tissue.

Dental Implant: a(usually) titanium cylinder surgically placed in the bone of the upper or lower jaw to replace the root of a missing tooth

Dental Prophylaxis: scaling an polishing procedure performed to remove coronal plaque, calculus, and stains. Usually performed by the Dental Hygienist.

Denture: removable complete set of upper or lower artificial teeth

Endodontist: A specialist who treats diseases of the tooth pulp (nerve chamber), performs Root Canals.

Extraction: Removal of a tooth.

Filling: Material used to fill a cavity or replace part of a tooth.

Fluoride: A chemical compound that helps strengthen teeth as well as reduce tooth decay and sensitivity.

Gingiva: gum tissue

Gum Disease: Gum disease (periodontal disease) occurs when plaque is allowed to build up on the teeth and the gums (also called the gingiva). Early gum disease, which is called gingivitis, causes red, swollen gums that bleed easily when brushed.

Immediate Denture: Full Denture constructed for placement immediately after removal of remaining natural teeth

Implant Denture: A denture which receives its stability and retention from a dental implant.

Molars: The back teeth that are designed for grinding food before swallowing

Night Guard: A removable acrylic appliance used to minimize the effects of grinding the teeth or joint problems, usually worn at night

Oral Surgeon: A dental specialist whose practice is limited to diagnosing and treating diseases, injuries, deformities and defects of the mouth.

Orthodontist: designs and applies corrective and supportive appliances, braces, to realign crooked teeth

Overdenture: denture that fits over tooth roots or dental implants

Palliative Treatment: treatment that is designed primarily to reduce or eliminate pain

Partial Denture: A removable appliance (prosthesis) that replaces some of the teeth in either the upper or lower jaw

Pedodontist: A dentist specializing in the treatment of children

Periodontal Disease: Gum disease.

Periodontist: a dental specialist whose practice is limited to the treatment of diseases of the supporting and surrounding tissues/gums of the teeth

Plaque: A sticky film on the teeth. If it is not removed by brushing it can harden into calculus.

Porcelain Fused To Metal (PFM) Crown: Full Crown with metal coping (for strength) covered by porcelain (for appearance).

Post-core: post and buildup to replace lost tooth structure and retain crown

Posterior Teeth: This refers to the premolar/bicuspids and molar teeth. The posterior teeth are those used for grinding food.

Prosthodontist: a dental specialist whose practice is limited to the restoration of the natural teeth and/or the replacement of missing teeth with artificial substitutes

R.C.T.; See Root Canal Therapy.

Reline: process of resurfacing the tissue side of a denture with new base material

Restoration: replacement of portion of a damaged tooth, usually with fillings and crowns.

Root Canal: A procedure used to save an abscessed tooth in which the pulp chamber is cleaned out, disinfected, and filled with a permanent filling

Sealants: Used to prevent tooth decay, sealants are a plastic liquid which is placed on the top surfaces of posterior teeth. The sealant hardens into place, forming a shallow surface that is easily cleaned with a toothbrush.

Sedative Base: Medication placed on top of pulp to help restore vitality of tooth.

Space Maintainer: dental device that holds the space lost through premature loss of baby teeth

Stainless Steel Crown; A pre-made metal crown, shaped like a tooth, that is used to temporarily cover a seriously decayed or broken down tooth.

About the Author

Ellen Broyles is a Registered Dental Assistant and has worked in the dental industry for over 25 years. She has worked in almost every specialty field as a dental assistant as well as working in the general dentistry office. Her specialty fields have included endodontics, orthodontics, oral surgery, periodontics and pedodontics. She has also been a dental assistant instructor. She has served with Northwest Medical/Dental Teams and Union Gospel Mission as a volunteer. Ellen is currently freelancing for dental offices in the King County area in Washington State. She is a personal dental consultant for dental patients who need advice with their dental needs and their dental insurance rights. She is also extremely honored to be working with Medical Teams International as their Mobile Dental Clinic Manager.

For more survival tips visit The Dental Patient's Survival Guide companion website at
www.survivingthedentist.com